Twilight Tours
The Illustrated Guide to the REAL Forks

Twilight Tours

The Illustrated Guide to the REAL *Forks*

by

George Beahm

with the Forks Chamber of Commerce

Underwood Books
Nevada City, CA

PUBLISHED BY UNDERWOOD BOOKS (www.underwoodbooks.com)

ISBN 978-1-59929-036-2 softcover   ISBN 978-1-59929-037-9 hardcover

First edition: August, 2009   10 9 8 7 6 5 4 3 2 1   Printed in China

Library of Congress Cataloging-in-Publication Data

Beahm, George W.
Twilight tours : the illustrated guide to the real Forks / by George Beahm with the Forks Chamber of Commerce.
p. cm.
1. Forks (Wash.)--Description and travel. 2. Forks (Wash)--Guidebooks. 3. Meyer, Stephenie, 1973- Twilight saga series--Miscellanea. I. Forks Chamber of Commerce. II. Title.
F899.F573B43 2009
917.97'99--dc22

Dedication

This one's for the good people of Forks, who made me feel welcome.

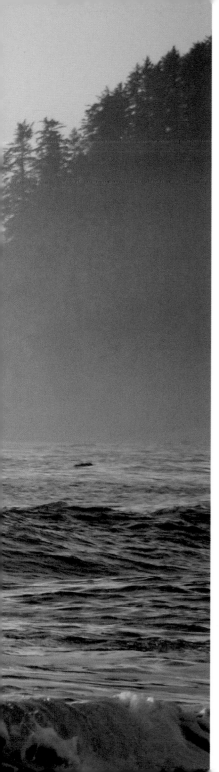

Table of Contents

The Olympic Mountains

Foreword
Forks–or Bust!

WHEN BELLA SWAN FLEW from Phoenix to Seattle, it was a jaunt of 1,453 miles. Southwest makes that non-stop flight in a little over three hours. My cross-country trip from Williamsburg, Virginia to Seattle spanned 2,950 miles and took seven hours.

The final leg of my air trip to Forks meant catching a shuttle to Boeing Field, a general aviation airport near Seattle's Sea-Tac Airport. I boarded a nine-seater, prop-driven plane from Kenmore Air to make the scenic hop on one of its daily flights to nearby Port Angeles, thirty minutes away as the eagle flies.

Flying at six thousand feet, high over the Olympic Mountains capped with snow, our plane descended into the William R. Fairchild International Airport west of Port Angeles, a city of nearly 20,000 people.

I got a car from Budget, one of only two car rental agencies serving the airport. Forks is 57 miles to the west. Hugging the base of mountains as the road twists and turns, Route 101 flanks Lake Crescent to the north. Once past the Lake, it's a clear shot to Forks, surrounded by distant mountains etched against the skyline.

Driving a small car with towering mountains around me, watching eighteen-wheelers rumbling down the road with full loads of harvested timber, I felt insignificant in comparison.

After a little more than an hour of driving, I passed La Push Road on my right, and I knew I was in the neighborhood. Had I hung a right on that road, I would have ended up on Quileute Indian land. Instead, I continued straight and passed clusters of buildings hugging the road. I crossed a steel-trestle bridge spanning the Calawah River. Off to my right, on a steep bluff, were two signs. In the foreground, a rectangular sign bore the legend: "The City of Forks Welcomes You." Behind it, a larger sign stated that Forks Outfitters was one mile ahead on the right.

Looking around at the rugged territory, I could easily imagine how the Cullens would range these mountains on foot. They likely stalk the wildlife that live in the nearby Olympic National Park, with its 922,651 acres studded with towering Douglas firs and Sitka spruce trees topping 200 feet. In these forests, the natural predators—the coyotes, cougars, and black bears—are outmatched by their unnatural predators, the vampires that called the small town of Forks home.

As I entered sunny Forks, my first impressions matched my mental snapshots: a small working-class town where sports utility vehicles and pick-up trucks dominated the streets and parking lots; where people necessarily dressed in warm, not fashionable, clothing; and where informality and friendliness characterize this town's social make-up. Simple and unpretentious, unlike life in fast-paced big cities, Forks offers a relaxed pace. The town seems to suggest: *Don't be in such a rush. Slow down and take it easy.*

I liked Forks immediately. With its population of 3175 people, Forks has a homey feel of a close-knit community that looks after, and takes care of, its own. For that reason, I was not surprised that many of the small retail stores in town posted rosters of their young men and women in the armed forces serving overseas in Iraq or Afghanistan. Across this country, in other small towns, similar rosters have gone up.

As an Army veteran of many years, I felt a hard lump in throat when I read all the names, because I knew that they won't all be coming back home. Make no mistake: the folks in Forks made sure *every* name is highlighted, *every* name is honored in those roll calls,

Seattle from the air

Sharing the road with logging trucks

Steel trestle bridge

My commuter plane

Signs north of town

because each service member could lay claim to a family with local roots going back several generations. *Every name counts.*

Mindful of the 30 mile-per-hour speed limit, I took in the town visually as I drove on its main route, Forks Avenue. I head to the Chamber of Commerce Visitor Center located south of the city in a rustic-looking building.

You can't miss the Visitor Center because it stands out from the road: a red pickup truck bearing a "Bella" license

Forks treeline

plate is parked out front. The Visitor Center is usually the first stop for Twilight Fans.

It's past lunchtime, though, and I'm hungry. There are plenty of affordable choices: pizza, hamburgers, steak, and fresh seafood, including salmon, a local specialty. For now, I pass on the Bella Burger (at Sully's Burgers), Bellasagna and Ed's Bread (at Pacific Pizza), and the other Twilight-themed foods. I head to John Harkel's place, the Forks Coffee Shop, prominently featured in Catherine Hardwicke's *Twilight: Director's Notebook*.

I seat myself and look at the menu with its plain, hearty food for folks with an appetite. My pancake is so large that it hangs over the plate. The second plate holds a generous side of crisp bacon and eggs. A cup of bottomless coffee helps wash it all down.

"The city of Forks welcomes you."

That's what the sign said when I entered the town.

It's a promise they keep. Welcome to Forks.

Twilight Tours

*The Illustrated Guide
to the REAL Forks*

Walking through a Storyteller's Dream
A town and book named Forks

AT THE VISITOR CENTER of the Chamber of Commerce in Forks, Washington, colored pins on large wall maps mark the hometowns of visitors who come here. Every state in the continental United States is dotted with pins; dozens more indicate visitors from around the world.

What draws thousands of predominantly female visitors of all ages to Forks? It's not the scenery, though it is breathtakingly beautiful: sea stacks rise in the fog offshore at La Push's First Beach, land that belongs to the Quileute Indians, their home for thousands of years. Nor is it the nearby Hoh Rain Forest, one of the few temperate zones in the world, where lush vegetation grows in profusion—it's part of the Olympic National Park, nearly a million

Facing page: Downtown Forks at night. *Above:* The map in the Visitor Center marks the hometowns of *Twilight* fans that have come to Forks.

square acres protected by the National Park Service.

The visitors come to Forks because of the vampires: specifically, the Cullen family. The key draw is Edward Cullen, born in Chicago in 1901, fixed in time at seventeen years of age. Inhumanly handsome, Edward Cullen is irresistibly drawn to an mortal girl named Isabella (Bella) Swan who has reluctantly returned to Forks to live with her divorced father.

Forks is a working-class town. Its main industry consists of two correctional facilities (Clallam Bay Correctional Center and Olympic Corrections Center) a short commute away. Once billed as the "logging capital of the world," that is largely its past; the future, in part, must embrace literary tourism, which owes everything to *Twilight*, a bestselling book by first-time author Stephenie Meyer.

The female visitors come to see the town where Bella Swan and Edward Cullen attend high school, where Dr. Carlisle Cullen tends to his patients, where an Indian named Jacob Black fulfills his destiny as a shape-shifting werewolf, and where the unusual Cullen family, recent transplants from Alaska, now live. The tourists come year-round to Forks to experience firsthand its fictional landscape.

Ranging in age from tweens to grandmothers, they also come to experience a meteorological anomaly: this small town is rained upon more than any other in the continental United States, which is why Stephenie Meyer chose to set *Twilight* here. Because her vampires' skin sparkles in sunlight like thousands of glittering diamonds, they prefer perpetually gloomy weather: rainy, overcast or mostly cloudy. (Forks is drenched with 120 inches of rain annually.)

Whether traveling on their own, with GPS units mounted in their cars, or on a minibus tour sponsored by a retail store appropriately named Dazzled by Twilight, the fans are crestfallen when the sun comes out: they want, and expect, to experience the rainy weather that characterizes everyday life in Forks. The rainy weather, after all, is when the vampires come out.

The fans come to experience *Twilight*'s book and movie magic, though no scenes from the movie were actually filmed in Forks — they were shot in nearby Oregon (Portland and St. Helens).

No matter. The *book* is set in Forks, and that's good enough for the fans. It's also good enough for the town's Chamber of Commerce, whose employees downplay the movie connection because they don't want to disappoint fans that show up expecting to see in Forks what they've seen on screen.

Remarkably, given that Stephenie Meyer did most of her research online, *Twilight*'s topography is largely accurate.

In July 2004, Stephenie and her older sister Emily retraced Bella Swan's route to Forks. Stephenie wrote about the experience on her official website (www.stepheniemeyer.com).

••

A Brigham Young University graduate with an English degree, Stephenie Meyer recalls exactly when the muse paid her a nocturnal visit. On June 2, 2003, Stephenie dreamt about a young couple in love, a seventeen-year-old girl named Bella Swan, and a deceptively young-looking boy named Edward Cullen. Inspired in part by Shakespeare's play *Romeo and Juliet*, she imagined a story of star-crossed lovers who live in completely different worlds: she's human and he's nonhuman; she's a mortal girl and he's a vampire who, at considerable odds with himself, resists mightily the temptation to indulge in his kind's traditional fare, human blood; in Edward's case, Bella's blood.

Bella, on the other hand, wants to forsake her human world and become one of the "cold ones," as the local Indians call them. Edward, though, wants Bella to live out her natural life. Moreover, Edward's concerned about her immortal soul, since he feels that being a vampire may condemn one to a life sentence of eternal damnation, with no possibility of salvation. This moral conundrum—should Edward turn Bella into a vampire with all its attendant risks despite her feelings?—is at the heart of the story.

Stephenie shared the work in progress with her older sister Emily, who encouraged her to continue. Writing quickly in moments stolen from taking care of her three young sons, Stephenie completed *Forks*, the 130,000 word novel, in three months. She then queried publishers and agents, including Writers House. Jodie Reamer at Writers House took her on as a client and helped fine-tune *Forks* into *Twilight*. Jodie subsequently shopped it around and hit the jackpot: Little, Brown and Company bought the rights to *Twilight* and two sequels in a $750,000 deal. The book publisher, sensing an entertainment franchise in the works, hoped it would turn out to be the wisest investment since Bloomsbury placed its bets on another first-time female author in her twenties who also wrote phone-book thick fantasy novels.

Twilight was published in hardcover on October 5, 2005. Among a sea of competing book covers in bookstores, *Twilight*'s visually arresting cover stood out because of its simplicity and elegance: A pair of female hands protectively cups a red apple. The photograph deliberately invokes biblical imagery: the fruit of forbidden knowledge and the moral dilemma of choice.

Little, Brown and Company's investment would soon pay off. Heralded as the new J.K. Rowling, Stephenie Meyer who, like her contemporaries, grew up online, tirelessly promoted herself on message boards, encouraged fan websites, built her own official website, and responded to readers' e-mails, until the sheer volume of queries proved overwhelming.

After tapping the power of the Web to spread the word about *Twilight*, Meyer soon followed its publication with sequels, each

Opposite: The Hoh Rain Forest, one of the world's few magnificent temperate zones.

Above: The Forks Timber Museum was one of the town's major tourist attractions for many years—that is, until the *Twilight* fans began to appear in increasing numbers.

with a strong graphic image set against a black background: a ruffled tulip for *New Moon*, and a broken silk ribbon for *Eclipse*.

In the summer of 2008, the Twilight phenomenon reached critical mass. Interest in the franchise intersected with the publication of an unrelated novel (*The Host*); the controversial fourth and final book in the Twilight saga, *Breaking Dawn*; and the long-expected and eagerly anticipated movie adaptation of *Twilight*.

Twilight, a modestly budgeted $37 million movie from

Above left to right: Author Stephenie Meyer; the cover for the bestselling *Twilight* novel; *Entertainment Weekly* helped fuel the *Twilight* fim fever; the final *Twilight* movie poster.

Summit Entertainment, was expected to make a small profit, but no one anticipated the pent-up fan demand that would soon propel ticket sales to the moon. The first clue that *Twilight* would be no run-of-the-mill movie manifested itself at the San Diego Comicon on July 24, 2008 when an estimated six thousand female fans assembled in a convention hall to get their first glimpse at the cast and crew.

As the supporting cast were introduced onstage, loud screaming erupted. Finally, the principals came out: Kristen Stewart, obviously a little uncomfortable by the brouhaha, walked out and the crowd screamed with enthusiasm. But when Robert Pattinson walked out, pandemonium erupted; the fans screamed even more wildly. Stephenie Meyer and Catherine Hardwicke were the last to take their seats.

When the moderator merely said, "Robert," the Pattinson fans again erupted with loud screaming. "I think you have a few fans out here! I can't even hear anything!"

But Hollywood heard those fans loud and clear: If this was any indication of what to expect from the collective Twilight fan base, the movie studio felt confident that the movie would be off to a respectable start on opening weekend. Possibly the fans would return for multiple viewings, a key factor in the success of *Titanic*, the biggest grossing movie in motion picture history.

Twilight began to command major attention from the world's media, anxious to report on what was clearly shaping up to be the Next Big Thing in pop culture.

Any doubts about *Twilight*'s success as a movie were put to rest by its impressive opening weekend gross of $69 million. Clearly, *Twilight* was on its way to the top of the charts.

Fueling the fervor, fan interest in Robert Pattinson soared.

The young actor who played Cedric Diggory in the Harry Potter movies would soon eclipse Harry Potter star Daniel Radcliffe in visibility. Understandably, Pattinson's response to his sudden fame was bewilderment, especially when young girls asked him to bite them, please! *I'm just an actor*, he probably thought, *so why all this fuss?*

Because they're simply crazy about Robert Pattinson as Edward Cullen.

In 2008 alone, over 22 million copies of the Twilight saga had sold. It didn't hurt that unlike most authors, Meyer is telegenic and at ease in front of the television camera; she comes across with warmth and humor and has a sense of perspective about her sudden success.

That same year, overwhelmed by a frenetic pace required to promote her books and movie, Stephenie was unable to complete *The Twilight Saga: The Official Guide*. Since the book had been prematurely announced, this was a major disappointment for her millions of fans. The book was rescheduled for September 2009.

After a very hectic 2008, Stephenie decided that it was time to let her creative well fill back up: She'd stepped away from the spotlight, away from the glare of the cameras, the insatiable fans and the omnipresent media. Instead of jetting around the world to fuel the star-making machinery that transformed a self-termed "insignificant little hausfrau" into a celebrity, she stayed at home and immersed herself in writing.

When the movie had run its course in movie theaters worldwide, *Twilight* racked up $376,336,500 million, according to boxofficemojo.com: ($191,453,148 domestically, $184,883,352 internationally). The movie franchise, off to an impressive start

Above: The cast for the *Twilight* film adaptation were met by 6000 fans at the San Diego Comic-Con International in 2008. *Below:* Downtown Forks. *Opposite:* Elisa Seaton and Lisa Jones flank a cardboard cutout of "Edward" (actor Robert Pattinson).

and now on a firm financial footing, scheduled *New Moon* in November 2009 and *Eclipse* in June 2010 (No decision has yet been made regarding the release of *Breaking Dawn.*)

In March 2009, the DVD release of *Twilight* sold 5.6 million copies in its first eight days—an impressive record.

••

No doubt the residents of Forks, who never dreamed their small town would appear in a bestselling book, have mixed feelings about the attention now focused on them. Some residents have grumbled about how their town's anonymity is forever gone—a reason why many novelists set their stories in fictitious towns—but others welcome the attention and the tourism that it brings.

One thing's for sure, though: Stephenie Meyer has forever changed Forks' visibility—she put it on the literary map, and in doing so made it visible to the entire world.

Forks is now adjusting to its newfound notoriety.

••

What draws the fans to Forks is its authenticity. Though the movie locations are set elsewhere, the town of Forks is the most indelible part of the Twilight landscape. It's where Twilight fans come to see the unreal become real, to step into the pages of their favorite novel and walk through a storyteller's dream, and to explore the literary landscape of a small town named Forks.

The Forks Chamber of Commerce
Visitor Center

Address: 1141 South Forks Avenue, Forks, WA 98331.
Mail: PO Box 1249, Forks, WA 98331.
Phone: 360-374-2531. Fax: 360-374-9253. E-mail: info@forkswa.com
Web: www.forkswa.com

A SIGN AT THE FORKS Chamber of Commerce Visitor Center announces, "Vampires thrive in Forks." How often are you going to see a sign that says *that* at any town's Visitor Center? Not often. But you'll find it here in Forks where the Cullens believe that the family that preys together stays together. The largest group of its kind (except for the Volturi in Volterra, Italy), the Cullens are necessarily close-knit and allow no outsiders in their inner circle, with one notable exception: a human girl named Bella Swan, smitten by one of their own, Edward Cullen.

Located on the south end of town, the Visitor Center is the logical starting point for any self-directed tour. Headed by Mike Gurling (Chamber Visitor Center Manager) and Marcia Bingham (Chamber Director), the Chamber's staff fields ques-

tions from Twilighters who arrive from all over the world to experience firsthand what Forks has to offer. When visiting, be sure to get Mike and Marcia's personal recommendations on lodging, food, shopping, and local sites; they are eager to share their in-depth knowledge of Forks and the surrounding locales to make your stay in town a memorable one.

Be sure to ask them about some of the wacky queries from prospective visitors planning a trip to Forks. (They've got some real doozies to pass along, including the call from a concerned fisherman who was reluctant to come to town during fishing season because he heard rumors about its vampire infestation.)

With free wireless connectivity to the Internet, public rest-rooms, and free coffee to perk up the weary traveler, the Visitor

Center caters to Twilight fans who want to explore the Cullen countryside.

Here are some travel tips for Twilighters:

1. Pick up a "Forks Twilight Map."

It's free, in full color and pocket-size, highlighted with key points of interest. It also has a list of places to find Twilight-related merchandise and a list of eateries where Twilight-related culinary delights will satisfy any appetite: the Bella Berry Pie, the Twilight Sandwich, the Bella Berry Smoothie, the Bellasagna with Ed's Bread (garlic, of course), Jacob's Blackberry Cobbler, and the famous Bella Burger.

Because Forks is a one-stoplight town with Route 101 running right down its middle, navigation is easy. Drive up and down the main drag to get a sense of place; park and take a walking tour of the shops and the eateries, especially the ones highlighted on the map. Merchants have gone out of their way to carry Twilight-related merchandise, much of it locally produced.

2. Pick up a restaurant guide: Forks' Bites!

A handy reference to all the eateries in and around Forks, this map is numbered with call-outs listing places with an abbreviated list of their specialties. Go ahead and sink your teeth into a "cullenary" dish. Take a bite—you know you can't resist.

3. Browse the Twilight "Lexicon," the scrapbooks.

Newspaper clippings and letters from fans worldwide make

Facing page: Marcia Bingham greets guests at the Visitor Center's gift shop. *Above left:* Elisa, Lisa, and Vampires thrive in Forks. *Above right:* North 101 road sign shows the way.

the scrapbooks essential reading. These fantastic scrapbooks are especially fun reading for newcomers who want to get an overview of the Twilight phenomenon.

4. Peruse the literature racks.

There's a wealth of information available about Forks and the local area in the pocket-sized brochures stacked in the racks, including many covering the Olympic National Park; packed with insider information, they are informative and illustrated.

One brochure, issued by the Olympic National Park, reminds travelers that they are "in Cougar country!" Though the brochure states that "attacks on humans are rare, but can occur," its advice, if attacked, is to "fight back aggressively." That's an important safety tip, so I'd make a mental note of that, just in case there's no Cullen around to help out.

5. Sign the guestbook.

Let others know where you are from and pen your thoughts in the book. The hometowns culled in the guestbook are highlighted with pins on giant wall maps.

6. Buy a souvenir from the shop.

For the non-Twilight fan back home whom you want to gift with a thoughtful souvenir, buy a postcard, photo, print, or book highlighting the magnificent landscape surrounding Forks. Twilight fans, of course, can get dressed to the nines with the Visitor Center's ample selection of locally produced tee-shirts, jerseys, pullovers and other apparel, priced from $16 to $40.

Don't worry if you've left town without your favorite Forks apparel; the good folks at the Visitor Center take web orders.

••

Now, keep on trucking; there's a lot of ground to cover. If it's raining, and you want to blend in with the locals who just grin and bear it, keep your umbrella in the car. And watch out for those cougars, black bears, and especially the Roosevelt Elk, who have been known to charge visitors if they get *too* close....

"Bella's" Red Pickup Truck

YOU CAN'T MISS IT: a rust-red Chevy pickup truck parked outside the Chamber of Commerce Visitor Information Center. The license plate is a dead giveaway: "BELLA."

Twilighters are frequently photographed in front of the repainted truck with its rusted grill. Its driving days are over, of course, but this particular vehicle has special significance for Stephenie Meyer fans. Every *Twilight* reader knows that Bella Swan is the proud owner of a Chevy pickup truck; it was a homecoming gift from her father Charlie, who bought it from his friend Billy Black.

As to the car's age, Stephenie Meyer notes in *Twilight* that it's a 1953 model. When Bella asks, though, Charlie sheepishly explains that it was "new in the early sixties—or late fifties at the earliest." Despite its age, it's in good shape mechanically, because Billy's son, Jacob, is a mechanical wizard who has spent a lot of time restoring it to road-worthy status. The truck's top speed, says Jacob, is 60 miles per hour.

The old red Chevy truck is the perfect vehicle for Bella, because it helps her blend in. Many of her classmates at Forks High School drive similar vehicles chosen for their utility, not their appearance.

For show, there's always the Cullens' cars. Edward drives a silver-colored Volvo S60 R to school, but picks her up in an Aston Martin V12 Vanquish when they go to the prom. Rosalie drives a red BMW M3 convertible. Emmett drives a Jeep Wrangler. (Alice is without wheels until Edward gifts her with a 911 Turbo Porsche.)

Bella, who was saving up to buy her own car, is happy that it's a purchase she doesn't have to make. The only thing that the Chevy truck lacks is a radio, which she receives as a birthday gift from the Cullens. (In *New Moon*, she claws it out after a falling out with Edward. A painful reminder, the empty hole in the dashboard of her truck symbolizes the one in her heart.)

Bella's lucky that her father got the truck for a song, because

it's considered a classic car, a favorite for restoration. With a peppy six cylinder engine and a four-speed manual transmission, large running boards, a wide bench seat, and a big cargo area in the back, these sturdy vehicles are still rocking and rolling, but they aren't bargains. (A fully restored Chevy truck of that vintage in fully restored condition can fetch up to $20,000.)

So what's inside the truck for Bella's comfort? Not much, except a bench seat and a heater. And the Delco radio, once state-of the art, is now ancient technology: push-button tuning came only on the deluxe model; the ordinary version came with a twist-knob. Its sole speaker blasts out monaural sound.

In *Twilight*, Bella describes her truck as "one of those solid iron affairs that never gets damaged—the kind you see at the scene of an accident, paint unscratched, surrounded by pieces of the foreign car it had destroyed."

For Bella, the truck represents personal freedom, for she no longer has to rely on friends, ride in her father's police car, or—when no other options are available—walk two miles to school.

And if she wants to drive to La Push or head out to Port Angeles for some serious shopping, she's got her own wheels. Without wheels in Forks, cabin fever is a certainty.

Now put yourself in the driver's seat. Imagine sitting in the cab and looking out of its expansive window. Imagine turning the key and cranking the engine as it comes to life with a distinctive, throaty roar. Imagine twisting or pushing that radio dial until you find a tune that puts you and your loving companion in the mood. Think Elvis Presley's "Love Me Tender" or "Unchained Melody" by The Righteous Brothers. Then head to La Push's First Beach at sunset....

If you're got some time on your hands afterward, head to Port Angeles for a bite. There's a restaurant called Bella Italia that serves a mouth-watering mushroom ravioli....

Facing page: Fans enjoy having their pictures taken next to "Bella's" pickup. *Below:* The Bella Italia in nearby Port Angeles offers great food in an intimate atmosphere.

The "Police Chief's" House
also known as the "Swan" house

Address: 775 K. Street, Forks, WA, 98331.
Status: No public access. It's the private residence of Kim and David McIrvin.
Notes: This is one of the few two-story homes in Forks, where the median house value in 2007 was $145,452. When the Chamber of Commerce asked if the McIrvins would allow it to stand-in for the Swan House, they kindly agreed. A prominently posted sign outside designates it as "The Swan House."

THE HOUSE SEEN IN the movie version of *Twilight* is a private residence (184 South 6th Street, Saint Helens, OR 97051), and closed to the public. As to why the filmmakers, who found Forks suitable for filming purposes, chose not to shoot there, the answer is simple: money. As Mark Cotta Vaz pointed out in *Twilight: The Complete Illustrated Movie Companion*, "Forks and its environs were the story, and had the requisite beautiful locations, but lacked the housing and infrastructure necessary for a movie crew on a tight budget."

••

The Police Chief in Forks, Charlie Swan was likely a rookie when he first joined the force. Given that public servants' salaries

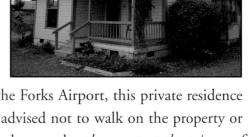

are typically well below those in the private sector, especially in a small town like Forks, the modest Swan residence is consistent with his modest salary.

Located in the south end of town, near the Forks Airport, this private residence is for show only; fans are advised not to walk on the property or ask to see its interior. In other words, *please respect the privacy of its owners.*

Forks Outfitters

Address: 950 South Forks Avenue, Forks, WA, 98331. Hours: 8 a.m. to 10 p.m. in the summer; 8 a.m. to 9 p.m. in the winter.
Web: www.forksthriftway.com.
Status: Open to the public.
Notes: Located in the south end of town off E. Street, this is the only shopping center in Forks, with three colocated stores: Thriftway, Ace Hardware, and Forks Outfitters. (There is an Olympic Outfitters, but not in Forks. Olympic Outfitters is located in Olympia, Washington. It was bought out in September 2008 by outdoors retailer Alpine Experience, also of Olympia.)

IN THE FICTIONAL WORLD of *Twilight*, Newton's Olympic Outfitters is owned by Mr. Newton, whose son Mike has an unrequited crush on Bella. Try as he might, Mike has *no* chance with Bella. It's a cruel fact of life that Mike must begrudgingly accept, since Bella is smitten with Edward Cullen.

Later, in *New Moon* and *Eclipse*, Bella talks about her part-time job at this store. She considers herself lucky that in this small town she was able to find any part-time work, because applicants far exceed the number of available positions.

In the real world of Forks, according to its website, Forks Outfitters has its roots dating back to 1951, when the Paul family bought the Forks Grocery and Feed. In 1961, the old building was razed and in its place Paul's Serve-U, a cement block building, was constructed. Subsequent improvements were made in 1973, adding the Forks Thrifty Mart, Ace Hardware, a Deli/Bakery, an Expresso Bar, and a new Service Center.

The sign outside the building complex, easily visible from the road, lists its stores: the Forks Outfitters ("The Original Outdoor

Store"), Thriftway ("Washington's Food Store"), and Ace Hardware. In recent years, a banner was added, announcing that this is "Twilight Headquarters" with "books, posters, gifts, shirts, hats, and more."

In Thriftway's entrance, a heavily trafficked area, a nearby corner caters to Twilight fans with an extensive assortment of Twilight memorabilia. Its "Twilight Headquarters" sells all the books (individual copies and the boxed set), the movie soundtrack and score, insulated coffee mugs, regular coffee mugs, posters, and a local line of apparel. My favorite souvenir from this store is an employee nametag that says: "Bella S., Employee of the Year."

Forks Outfitters is well stocked with a wide selection of sporting goods: fish and tackle, camping equipment, maps, bait, hunting supplies, rain gear, camouflage clothing, sports supplies, shoes and boots, and durable work clothes.

Forks Outfitters also carries additional Twilight-themed hats, beanies, shirts, sweatshirts, hoodies, blankets, and throws: Team Edward; Team Jacob; Fang Club; Forks • WA; Spartans: Forks High School; Vampire Capital of the World: Forks, Washington; Love at First Bite, Forks • WA; Road Trip: What Happens in Forks, Stays in Forks, and more.

For fans staying locally, a trip to Forks Outfitters is essential: a one-stop shop for food, clothing and hiking supplies (for walks through the Hoh Rain Forest or First Beach at La Push). When you leave, stop by its espresso bar for a hot beverage—the perfect pick-me-up on a rainy day.

The Twilight Department

Forks Hospital

Street location: 503 Bogachiel Way, Forks, WA, 98331.
Tour Status: A working hospital, it's open to the public for medical emergencies *only*.
Notes: The reserved parking space for Dr. Cullen can be found adjacent to the hospital's emergency entrance.

THERE'S A RESERVED PARKING space for Dr. Cullen—that's Carlisle Cullen, the head of the family—at Forks Community Hospital, but his space remains vacant. You'll not find his car, a Mercedes S55 AMG, parked there. But if a black Mercedes happened to pull into the parking lot, Twilighters' heads would turn and their eyes would light up if a tall, blonde-haired, good-looking man emerged. (Born in 1645, Carlisle Cullen's physical appearance is that of a 23 year-old man.)

According to Police Chief Swan, in a conversation with his daughter Bella, recounted in *Twilight*, nurses at the hospital found the good doctor a handsome distraction.

Dr. Cullen is unique among the staff at Forks Community Hospital; indeed, unique among the world's physicians, as he's probably the only vampire doctor in existence.

Given that vampires are immortal, Carlisle Cullen had time on his hands after crossing over from mortal to immortal. Carlisle used his time wisely, spending centuries to improve his medical knowledge. His hope was that with enough research, he'd find a way to wean himself away from human blood. The research paid off. He and his family are able to subsist on animal blood. A "vegetarian" vampire (as the Cullens describe themselves), Carlisle is a living contradiction: Rather than take life, he restores it; and rather than claim victims, he saves them, always mindful of the implications of the Hippocratic Oath: To the best of his considerable abilities, he will be a life-giving, not life-taking, force for the good of all.

As Edward Cullen explained to Bella, as recounted in *Twilight*, "... But Carlisle has always been the most humane, the most compassionate of us...I don't think you could find his equal throughout all of history."

Because of their bloodthirsty nature, vampires wrestle with their moral conscience. Edward Cullen, for instance, wonders if he's a damned creature, one without a soul, who will never be redeemed in God's eyes. It is the nature of the beast.

Dr. Cullen, unlike his adopted son Edward, has no time to torture himself with such philosophical musings. There are always patients to see, patients to save, and survivors to comfort. Playing the devil's advocate, one muses: If vampires are eternally damned, can they redeem themselves by their good work? Does Dr. Cullen deserve consideration for rising above his fellow vampires by not succumbing to the "thirst," the lust for blood?

If there's any justice in this world, Dr. Cullen, who may have begun his dark journey through hell as a budding vampire, may have redeemed himself by leaving it a better place than which he found it. In the grand scheme of things, surely Carlisle's efforts count if there's any divine mercy in the universe.

FORKS COMMUNITY
HOSPITAL

FORKS COMMUNITY HOSPITAL

← LONG TERM CARE ENTRANCE
← PHYSICAL REHABILITATION
← COMMUNITY HEALTH RESOURCE CENTER
← ADMINISTRATION BUILDING
↑ SURGERY PATIENT PICKUP
↑ HOSPITAL MAIN ENTRANCE
↑ EMERGENCY ENTRANCE
↑ URGENT CARE
↑ WEST END OUTREACH SERVICES

Forks High School

Address: 411 S. Spartan Ave., Forks, WA, 98331.
Web: www.forks.wednet.edu.
Status: off limits to non-students, faculty or staff during the school year; open by arrangement on special days to the general public.
Notes: The sign outside the school says "Forks High School," as does a sign in the back of the school. The sign over its front entrance states "Quillayute High School."

THE SCHOOL USED IN the *Twilight* film was James Madison High School (Portland, Oregon) for the interior shots and Kalama High School (Kalama, Washington) for exterior shots.

Pivotal movie scenes included Bella going to school for the first time, a scene of her nearly getting crushed by a van driven by another student, the cafeteria scene in which she first sees the Cullens, and a classroom scene in which she sits next to Edward in biology class, after which he inexplicably bolts.

The prom, the key scene of the novel, is set in the high school's gymnasium. As Bella notes, "In Phoenix, they held proms in hotel ballrooms. This dance was in the gym, of course. It was probably the only room in town big enough for a dance."

The gymnasium is in fact the only room in town big enough to hold hundreds of people for any function.

••

In 2007 Forks' high school's student body consisted of 309: 41 American Indian/Alaskan Natives, 2 Blacks, 45 Hispanics, and 221 Caucasians. (When Bella attended Forks, its student body, including herself, was 357.)

Another example of small town cohesiveness: A scholarship is available to any graduate for the asking. The fund, started in 1964, has raised over a million dollars to date.

Eric McHenry: Are people visiting the school on a daily basis in large numbers?

Forks High School principal Kevin Rupprecht: Pretty much. We'll walk out onto the street and see them standing in front of our building, taking pictures by the sign. And you can count on a large number of fans coming during breaks. Spring break was huge last year. And because it's staggered when different schools around the country take their breaks, we had it for about two months solid—just an astronomical number of people coming by, taking pictures and walking through the school. During the summer, there are people every single day. School's not in session, obviously, but there's still some staff around, and they come up and knock on the door, and we let them in and say hi and show them around. Last year, the city dedicated September 13 as Stephenie Meyer Day, and we opened up the school for Twilight tours. And we had hundreds of people coming to the building that day.

—(*Columns*, an alumni magazine published by the University of Washington)

The Police Station

Address: 500 E. Division Street, Forks, WA, 98331.
Web: www.forkswashington.org
Status: Open to the public on a limited basis.
Notes: There are eight officers on duty.

THE CURRENT FORKS CHIEF of Police answers not only to his name, Mike Powell, but increasingly to his alter-ego, the fictional Police Chief Charlie Swan, Bella's father. Powell, a graduate of Northwestern University, has over 22 years in Law Enforcement, so he knows Forks, its environs, and its people well.

The Forks City Hall, which includes the Police Station as part of its compound of buildings, is one of the featured stops on the "Dazzled by Twilight" minibus tour.

The Forks Police Department is comprised of five divisions: patrols (running 24/7), investigations (major crimes, investigations), CSO (Community Service Officer), Communications Center (operates 24/7 with enhanced 911 capability), and a jail housing 30 inmates.

Crime, as you'd expect in a small city, is minimal because strangers stand out, locals know their neighbors, and they look out after one another. The crime statistics back that up: from 2001 to 2007, for instance, there were no murders.

••

In the fictional movie *Twilight* universe, Police Chief Swan's many duties include investigations into a sudden rash of unexplained deaths, including Grisham Mill, where a worker is mauled to death. It clearly doesn't look like an industrial accident; rather, it looks like a wild animal attack. But it wasn't. It was the depredations of a band of roving vampires, headed up by James, accompanied by Laurent and Victoria. Unknowingly encroaching on Cullen territory, James and company are vampires who feast exclusively on human blood.

As they claim victims among the local population, including

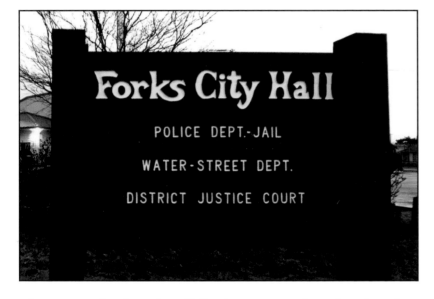

a boater at a local marina, Bella shows up on James's radar when he and his fellow predators go to investigate the unmistakable sounds of the Cullens playing baseball. What James discovers is that this chance encounter would offer him his most challenging hunt to date—Bella. To capture his prey, whom he derisively calls "a snack," he's got to be a survivor type and outwit, outplay, and outlast the Cullens. The hunt is on....

The Miller Tree Inn
also known as the "Cullen" house

Address: 654 E. Division St., Forks, WA, 98331.
Website: www.millertreeinn.com
Notes: This is a bed-and-breakfast with eight guest rooms. Located just down the street from the police station, the owners of Miller Tree Inn have allowed their house to stand in for the Cullen house.
Photo tip: The best pictures can be taken at dusk when the house lights are on.

YOU CAN'T MISS THE house: the mail box on the road is clearly labeled **CULLENS**.

Because there are usually guests staying at the B&B, the owners understandably discourage tourists from coming inside, because it's disruptive to their guests; however, you can walk the grounds and take pictures. Be sure to read the handwritten sign near the front entrance that explains why they are not in; messages change on a regular basis. For example: "Under the direction and supervision of my dear Carlisle, we have all gone to our local blood bank to volunteer. Our overnight guests will be cared for by our resident innkeepers, as usual. Thanks, Esme." (Let's hope Jasper sits *that* one out.)

Built in 1916, the white, three-story house has enough rooms for the Cullens.

Unlike the house described by Bella in *Twilight*, (rectangular and hidden by the forest), the stand-in house is boxy and partially hidden by trees.

••

The Cullen house seen in the *Twilight* movie is actually located in Portland, Oregon. A contemporary design, it is a private residence owned by a Nike executive who would like to enjoy his privacy, now that the on-site filming for the *Twilight* movie is history. (For photos of his striking house, see page 94 of Mark Cotta Vaz's *Twilight: The Complete Illustrated Movie Companion*.)

Under the direction and supervision of my dear Carlisle, we have all gone to our local Blood Bank to volunteer.
Our overnight guests will be cared for by our resident innkeepers, as usual.   Thanks, Esme

Dazzled by Twilight

Address: 61 N. Forks Avenue, Forks, WA 98331 † 135 E. First Street, Port Angeles, CA 98362.
Web: www.dazzledbytwilight.com and www.myspace.com/dazzledinforks
Phone: (360) 374-5101 for Forks; (360) 452-8800 for Port Angeles.
Email: annette@dazzledbytwilight.com
Status: Retail store, visitors welcome; open seven days a week from 10 a.m. to 6 p.m, or by special appointment for nocturnal types.
Notes: The only store of its kind in the world, this retail shop carries only Twilight memorabilia. (A satellite store is in nearby Port Angeles.)

"I truly love these books. For whatever reason, I found life-changing messages in them: love and family and dedication and sacrifice. I'm astonished at how many other people found *Twilight* life-changing. I love what I'm doing. It speaks to the heart and gives people a commonality that is very comforting. It's like a party here every day because it's fun."

— *Annette Root, Dazzled by Twilight store owner*

THE STORE CONDUCTS DAILY Twilight tours, available by appointment only. (The Forks Chamber of Commerce originally started the tours but handed this franchise over in March 2009 because of time constraints.)

The daily tour costs $39 per person—a bargain. A minimum of five people must book for an outing:

- The Breaking Dawn Tour starts at 8:00 A.M. It includes a cinnamon bun and a hot or cold beverage.
- The Volturi Tour starts at 11:30 A.M. It includes a Swan sandwich with chips and a beverage.
- The Twilight Tour starts at 3:00 P.M. It includes an Edward sundae or a milk shake—your choice of a Jacob Black shake or

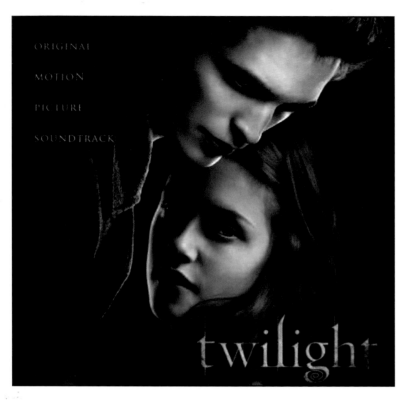

Above: The film soundtrack has proven popular with fans and features tracks by such bands as Muse, Paramore, and Linkin Park. *Opposite:* Dazzled by Twilight.

Vampire shake.

• The Midnight Sun Tour starts at 6:30. It includes an Edward sundae or a milk shake—your choice of a Jacob Black shake or a Vampire shake.

••

The merchandise at Dazzled by Twilight is impressive and extensive. (Dare I say dazzling?) A one-stop shop for Twilight fans, a partial list of merchandise—licensed and locally produced—include: the Twilight books (paperback and hardback, and boxed), the official movie companion, the Hardwicke

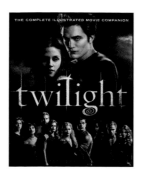   

Opposite and above: Whether they're interested in books, dolls, or jewelry, *Twilight* fans have a wide selection of merchandise to choose from.

movie diary book, the soundtrack, the music score, the *Twilight* DVD, school apparel from Forks High School, tote bags, framed movie posters, wall calendars, framed photographs of surrounding areas, Twilight themed road signs, apparel, black towels, handmade household goods, perfumes and lotions, apple paperweights, metal toy cars (a silver Volvo S60 R and a 1953 Chevy Truck), tote bags, baseball caps, life-size cardboard stand-ups of the key cast, rolled up movie posters, decals, music by artists who contributed to the soundtrack, buttons with Twilight references, pens, decals, wooden signs with characters' names, locally made jewelry, small sculpture, and a colored vase with flowers.

The store constantly gets in new inventory; ask if you don't see what you want and they can probably get it for you.

A labor of love, Dazzled by Twilight is heaven for Twilight fans and a haven for store owner Annette Root, who specifically moved to Forks to set up shop. Touched by the books and never wanting them to end, she envisioned creating a Disneyesque environment where Twilight fandom is celebrated.

Dazzled by Twilight is an immersive retail experience, with Twilight music piped through the store speakers, large posters of the book covers and movie posters on display, with red-and-black colored memorabilia everywhere. (The two colors symbolize Twilight.)

Release parties, themed to high-profile merchandise, draws very large crowds. The March 20, 2009 release of *Twilight* on DVD drew an estimated 600 fans. (The *Peninsula Daily News* reported that one attendee, visibly pregnant, wore a tee shirt that said, "Half vampire," with an arrow pointing to her belly. The mother-to-be has already picked out a name for her girl—Isabella, in honor of Bella Swan.)

If you want Twilight memorabilia, this is an essential stop if you're in Forks, in Port Angeles, or just surfing online.

The Hoh Rain Forest

THE NEED FOR ANIMAL sustenance necessitates that the Cullen family live where wildlife is plentiful. This may be a major reason why the family relocated to Forks, close to the federally protected Olympic Nature Park, with its population of black bear, Roosevelt elk, blacktail deer, cougars, bobcats, coyotes, snowshoe hares, short-tailed weasels, river otters and raccoons.

The Cullens are careful to cull the herd selectively; otherwise, they'd deplete the food supply. So when Bella asks about Edward's excursion to Goat Rocks (a wilderness area encompassing 107,018 acres in southwest Washington), he responds: "...we have to be careful not to impact the environment with injudicious hunting. We try to focus on areas with an overpopulation of predators—ranging as far away as we need. There's always plenty of deer and elk here, and they'll do, but what's the fun in that?"

What fun indeed?

••

Addresses:

Peak 6 Tours & Gift Shop (4883 Upper Hoh Road, Forks, WA 98331). Telephone: 360-374-5254.

Hard Rain Cafe (5763 Upper Hoh Rd, Forks, WA 98331). Telephone: 360-374-9288. Anna and Christian Matsche, owners.

For hardy travelers, explorers, and serious hikers, the National Parks in Washington state offer countless miles of trails to explore. Before setting out, however, be sure to get in shape physically and read up on what to expect. A good place to start is www.wilderness.net, which offers time-tested guidance and also lists the various fees and permits involved. It also provides numerous links for more information and photos.

Twilight fans pressed for time may want to retrace Stephenie Meyer's walk through the nearby Hoh Rain Forest. The only way to get there from Forks is south on Route 101. Take a left at the turnoff for the Olympic National Park. Take Upper Hoh Road until it ends, at the parking lot of the Visitor Center.

There are two retail stores to stock up on supplies and souvenirs: Peak 6, which can outfit you from head to toe in gear appropriate for the higher altitudes; a little further down the road,

the Hard Rain Cafe offers a mouth-watering selection of grilled food, and there's plenty of souvenirs to take home, too. (The Cafe's specialty is its intimidating half-pound "Mount Oly burger," layered with Swiss cheese, bacon, lettuce, tomato, onion, pickles, and a special sauce.)

The Hoh Rain Forest Visitor Center offers mostly printed product for sale: books, maps, bookmarkers, photos, etc. It also has exhibits, dioramas, static displays, and free brochures.

During the winter, take advantage of its wood-stoked stove, the ideal way to warm yourself up.

Admission to the park is $15 per vehicle. Keep in mind that during the summer, attendance mushrooms dramatically and the walking trails can be crowded.

There are several free maps highlighting the walking trails for every skill level: for the inexperienced, the manageable Hall of Mosses (with its 100 foot elevation gain), and the Spruce Nature Trail; hardier folk with more time and endurance will want to step out on the South Snider-Jackson (11.8 miles, ascending to 2,700 feet, with river crossings) or the Hoh River walk (17.3 miles

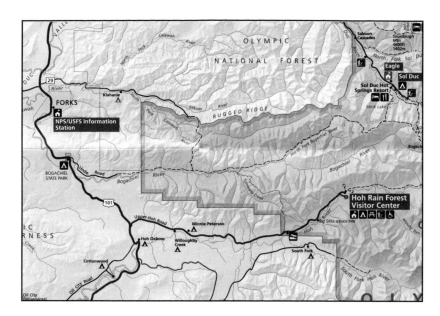

Opposite page: The park's rustic visitor center is dwarfed by the surrounding trees. *Above:* The map to the Hoh Rain Forest and a trail sign to help hikers plan their journey.

with a total elevation gain of 3,700 feet).

The park brochure states that backpackers "must obtain a wilderness camping permit" and that "Climbing Mount Olympus requires glacier travel skills and equipment."

As for the natural predators, bears, elk, and cougars are present and should be treated with respect. The bears are emboldened by the prospect of food, the elk have been known to charge tourists who get within 200 feet, and cougar sightings are possible but not probable.

The black bear, reared up on its hind feet, can tower seven feet tall. Weighing up to 660 pounds, it can run up to 30 miles per hour. In comparison, a young teenage male in good physical condition can only run 23 miles per hour in short spurts.

Roosevelt elk can stand up to five feet high and grow up to ten feet long; the bulls weigh up to 1,100 pounds and sport antlers.

A cougar, also called puma or mountain lion, is a big cat weighing 145 pounds. An exceptionally fast and agile predator, it can sprint up to 40-45 miles per hour, leap 16 feet vertically, and 45 feet horizontally. And it can also swim. No wonder Theodore Roosevelt termed this predator the "lord of stealthy murder." Fortunately, says the park service, "attacks on humans are rare, but can occur." Reassuringly, the park service says "few people will ever see a cougar."

The bears and cougars usually occupy higher terrain, but elk sightings are commonplace. I spied one walking majestically across the parking lot, ignoring cars and gawkers alike.

Travel tips: Bring a sturdy walking stick. And be sure to bring rain gear, just in case it rains.

La Push

"No Vampires Beyond This Point" *

Address: 320 Ocean Drive, PO Box 67, La Push, WA 98350.
Telephone 360-374-5267 and 1-800-487-1267.
Web: www.quileutenation.org
Important Safety Note: Thrill-seekers should be aware of the fact that there is no such thing as cliff-diving in La Push—it's merely a storytelling device in *New Moon*. As Forks native Anna Matsche explains, "beneath the sea stacks, the water is turbulent. There's no way of knowing if the water you're diving into has a submerged sea stack or not."

SEA STACKS, LIKE JAGGED teeth, jut up offshore La Push. As the sun sets, a thin blanket of fog lays over the cove harboring dozens of modern fishing boats. Traditionally a seafaring people, the Quileutes venture out to catch salmon and steelhead, but they no longer paddle out in long wooden canoes; they pilot watercraft outfitted with powerful diesel engines.

Today, tourism is the Quileute Nation's major industry. Once encompassing 900 square miles, its territory has shrunk down to a single square mile. The population numbers in the hundreds. Their native language, spoken only by village elders, is complex. Few speak it, and when the elders pass on, their colorful language faces extinction: unique words like *álita* (fish), *káya* (water), *kíkit* (elk).

••

Of all the places on the Twilight tour of Forks, this is my favorite because it's where history and Twilight fiction intersect:

A prominent sign erected near a grocery store at the intersection of La Push Road and Mora Road, near the Quileute Nation at La Push.

though the Quileutes have nothing in their tribal stories regarding vampires, the stories regarding men descended from wolves is part of their culture.

Carlisle Cullen, born in 1640, is well known to the Quileutes, as Jacob explained to Bella as they walked on La Push's First Beach: "So my great-grandfather made a truce with them. If they would promise to stay off our lands, we wouldn't expose them to the palefaces."

The truce frayed when Bella entered the picture, setting into motion a chain of events that potentially put it at risk. It would pit vampires against their hereditary enemies, werewolves, and create an irreparable rift.

Bella's connection to the Quileutes is through a family friend, Billy Black, a senior member of the Quileute tribal council. A grandson of Ephraim Black, considered to be the last true Quileute leader, it's Billy who tells his son Jacob about "the cold ones."

It's Jacob that in so many ways is inextricably linked to Bella. It's Jacob who suffers from unrequited love; he's the third person in a romantic triangle with Bella and Edward. Jacob is also her best friend, protector and life-saver. As a shape-shifting Alpha werewolf forced into a leadership role (a birthright that he initially denied), he proves to be instrumental to Bella's safety: Victoria, a rogue vampire on the hunt for Bella, lost her mate James to Edward, who killed him in a battle while trying to protect Bella. She now wants to even the score by killing Bella.

Above: The sign announcing your arrival in La Push. *Opposite:* The fog-enshrouded La Push Harbor offered a moody photo opportunity.

••

Tourism is the Quileute Nation's best prospect for a bright economic future, especially since they will take center stage in the film adaptation of *New Moon*, when the Cullens leave Forks and Bella seeks solace from Jacob Black.

Tourists who come to La Push will find a beachfront resort that offers unique insights of local Indian culture through its gift shop, tribal ceremonies, and storytelling events.

Lodging in La Push is affordable ($95 to $280), with a wide selection: townhouses, duplex units, luxury cabins, and the new

Thunderbird Motel. Forks local Anna Matsche explains, "When people come to the oceanfront, they expect higher end accommodations. They don't want bare-bones lodging; they want amenities. The Resort has beautiful cabins that are out of sight from the road. They've put a lot of thought into them. They had an architect that designed aborigine-inspired buildings, and he incorporated a lot of styles and symbols from the Indian culture. The cabins are quite beautiful."

If you want to get away from the grind of civilization, La Push's Oceanside Resort is a great escape. Whether it's kayaking, surfboarding, whale-watching, or taking long walks on the beaches, La Push is an essential Twilight destination.

VAMPIRES OND THIS POINT

Port Angeles, Washington

Web: www.portangeles.org

WHEN FORKS RESIDENTS WANT "to go to the big city," as Forks local Anna Matsche says, they go to nearby Port Angeles to the movies, to dine at upscale restaurants with fine wine lists, or to shop for specialty items. Port Angeles is where the Strait of Juan De Fuca separates Washington State from nearby Canada; a short ferry ride connects the two.

When visiting Port Angeles, take a side trip to Victoria, B.C. Be sure to bring your passport, though; you'll need it when entering Canada and reentering the United States.

With a population of 18,789 (2007 census), Port Angeles is approximately six times the size of Forks. According to the Port Angeles Downtown Association, "Port Angeles found prosperity as a logging town, and as a natural deepwater port. ... As the economic structure of the area changed, Port Angeles responded by expanding its tourism base as an international gateway for travelers to Vancouver Island, British Columbia, and to the beautiful Olympic National Park."

The downtown area is where the commercial shops are located.

••

It's a short drive of approximately one hour from Forks to Port Angeles. It's a necessary trip for Bella's friends, who are shop-

A tall ship in the Port Angeles harbor

ping for prom dresses; Bella is planning to sit that event out, because of her innate clumsiness. "Both Jessica and Angela seemed surprised and almost disbelieving when I told them I'd never been to a dance in Phoenix," said Bella in *Twilight*.

The three women go to the only place in town with a wide selection of prom dresses. "Jess drove straight to the one big department store in town, which was a few streets in from the bay area's visitor-friendly face."

Address: 200 W. First Street, Port Angeles, WA, 98362.

Web: www.gottschalks.com

A regional department store chain with 59 department stores and three specialty stores in the west, Gottschalks filed for bankruptcy in January 2009. Its Port Angeles store, writes *Peninsula Daily News* reporter Tom Callis, "had the reputation of being the highest producer per square foot of all the company's stores in Washington state."

Though not specifically named by Bella in *Twilight*, the Gottschalks department store on First Street is the only place where Bella's friends could have shopped for prom dresses. Within walking distance, down the same street, is the bookstore Bella mentions, and a restaurant called La Bella Italia.

Port Book and News

Address: 104 E. First Street, PO Box 1543, Port Angeles, WA 98362. Tel: 360-452-6367.

Hours: Monday through Saturday, 8 a.m. to 8 p.m. Sunday, 9 a.m. to 5 p.m.

Web: www.portbookandnews.com

Note: In the novel *Twilight*, Bella doesn't visit any bookstore. In the movie version, she visits Thunderbird and Whale: New and Used Books.

••

"I had no trouble finding the bookstore," says Bella, "but it wasn't what I was looking for. The windows were full of crystals, dreamcatchers, and books about spiritual healing. I didn't even go inside. ... There had to be a normal bookstore in town."

This is the "normal" bookstore in town. An independent bookseller, Port Book and News carries "over 75,000 new and used books, maps, greeting cards, and other book-related items." On a wintery day in February, I popped in and combed the shelves of books. The mixture of new and used books, all neatly arranged on bookshelves, made browsing a delight.

Port Book and News also sponsors literary events held at the local library.

Why not stop by and ask for a personal recommendation for a book by a local author or photographer? The staff is happy to help you find that perfect book for yourself or someone back home.

Bella Italia

Address: 118 E. First Street, Port Angeles, WA 98362.
Hours: seven days a week, opening at 4:00 p.m.
Web: www.bellaitaliapa.com

After being saved from local thugs by the unexpected appearance of Edward Cullen, Bella Swan is understandably shaken by the close encounter. She joins Edward for an impromptu dinner date at La Bella Italia.

It's their first date, and Bella is not happy by the mesmerizing effect Edward has on the restaurant's hostess and their waitress, both of whom treat Bella Swan as an ugly duckling. They ignore her but shower attention on Edward. This unwelcome behavior prompts Bella to ask Edward if he's aware of the dazzling effect he has on others. (He's not.)

Bella automatically orders the first thing she sees on the menu, the mushroom ravioli. She slowly regains her composure after nibbling on breadsticks and sucking down two ice-cold

Cokes at Edward's urging. (Requiring neither food nor drink, Edward declines to partake.)

••

Stephenie Meyer, who visited the restaurant in June 2008, gave it her seal of approval. A group photo of Meyer and the restaurant's employees is prominently displayed in the storefront window. "And now Bella Italia is proud to be the Official 'TWILIGHT' restaurant in Port Angeles...."

Bella Italia is open for dinner only. It is known for the excellence of its wine list. Twilight fans will obviously want to try its signature Twilight dish—mushroom ravioli.

Hungry fans, though, have plenty of mouth-watering alternative choices. The restaurant's full menu is extensive with traditional Italian dishes and locally harvested seafood.

For an appetizer, try the grilled Portobello mushroom ($10) or the Bruschetta (Tuscan bread with garlic, olive oil, fresh basil, and Roma tomatoes; $10). There's enough to share, of course, between two hungry diners.

Entrees include pasta, beef, and seafood dishes.

Since fresh seafood is always a treat, try Pesci Di Giorno ("fresh local fish grilled or pan-seared, served with local organic vegetables, and Chef David's famous risotto"). But if you absolutely *must* have pasta, there's spaghetti, manicotti, salmon ravioli, lasagna, fettuccine, linguine, pizza, and other dishes.

If you're not a wine expert, ask for a recommendation. By the glass or the bottle, a good wine adds just the right touch to every meal. Local restaurant critics, the Kalebergs, have high praise for Bella Italia, especially its wine list. "Ask for the Riserva list and don't hesitate to talk to the staff about the wine. The list is particularly strong in Washington and Oregon reds. Everybody knows about Oregon's lovely pinot noirs, but Washington has delectable cabernet francs, soft merlots, and cabernet sauvignons that taste like ripe blackberries."

Leave room for cordials and dessert, though; they're a perfect way to cap off a memorable meal.

Epilogue
Forever Seventeen

THE FINAL SCENE IN the novel *Twilight* features Bella and Edward at the Forks High School gymnasium, where the prom is being held. The belle of the ball is Isabella, who is literally swept off her feet by Edward: he lifts her up and places her feet on top of his, so that he can dance for both of them. Bella, who has never known the exhilarating experience of ballroom dancing, admits it isn't "half bad."

It's Bella's way of conceding that she erred in giving Edward a severe tongue-lashing as they drove to the dreaded prom—the beauty (the mortal girl) and the beast (the immortal vampire).

Like Bella, her contemporaries are young adults with the potential of their whole lives ahead of them. It's Bella's mortal life, with all its attendant joys and sorrows, that Edward feels she should experience—it's her birthright. Bella, on the other hand, is ready to become a vampire that very night and lusts for Edward to transform her.

Edward has gone a lifetime surrounded by pairs of loving cou-ples (Carlisle and Esme, Jasper and Alice, Emmett and Rosalie). He gradually realizes that spending an eternity with-out love would be existentialist. But Edward realizes that he must protect Bella from herself, that he must dissuade her from wanting to become immortal for her own sake. He accepts the transitory nature of her mortal life, and promises to stay by her side until her natural end. He will then be alone once again.

•••

In the movie version of *Twilight*, filmed at The View Point Inn overlooking the Columbian River Gorge, Robert Pattinson and Kristen Stewart as Edward and Bella are dancing under an outdoor gazebo illuminated by hundreds of small lights. As the other couples drift away, leaving Edward and Bella to dance the night away, they are alone: two souls that miraculously found each other in a vast and uncaring universe.

It's a point in time symbolizing their perfect love: the past is

a distant memory, the future is light years away, but they live for, and cherish, this magic moment.

If you're lucky, you remember a similar moment in your past; if you're not, you surely wish to experience it, if only once in your life.

Each of us yearns to be one with another soul, someone special until the end of our days, because the alternative—a lifetime without love—is too monstrous to contemplate: it is no life at all.

This magic moment symbolizing undying love is at the timeless heart of *Twilight*. It's a story so universal that it touches women of all ages, from tweens to grandmothers in their seventies. It is, simply, the spiritual power of transformative love.

My favorite anecdote, recounted by Mark Cotta Vaz in *Twilight: The Complete Illustrated Movie Companion*, is one that film director Catherine Hardwicke shared with him: "[She] noted that for all the inherent darkness that came with vampires, it was the love story that touched people."

Said Hardwicke: "People of all ages are looking for a perfect love. People have read these books and been inspired to get out there!"

Adds Vaz: "Even her mother, in her seventies, had been taking art classes and thinking of switching to biology to see if she could get a lab partner like Edward."

••

If this unlikely couple—a mortal girl and a vampire boy—can find eternal love in a tiny town like Forks, it gives every *Twilight* reader hope that someday, somehow, love may blossom in her life as well.

As for Bella and Edward's fairy tale, did they live happily ever after? Go read *New Moon*, *Eclipse*, and *Breaking Dawn* to enjoy finding out for yourself.

And on that note, I take my leave. Thank you for coming along on my Twilight tour of a small town named Forks.

—*George Beahm*

The View Point Inn (40501 E. Larch Mountain Road, Corbett, OR 97019. Phone: 503-695-5811).
Website: www.theviewpointinn.com.

Because a high school gym decorated for a prom didn't have the romantic ambiance that *Twilight* film director Catherine Hardwicke envisioned, she went looking for an alternative and fortuitously found The View Point Inn. From its website: "This 1924 Nationally Registered Oregon landmark boasts a rustic upscale charm with a dramatic panoramic view of the entire Columbia River Gorge. The historic boutique hotel and fine dining restaurant is nestled high on a bluff overlooking the majestic Columbia River with breaktaking sunsets and the sparkling evening lights of Portland and Vancouver."

For *Twilight* fans, the View Point Inn has a special resonance because it is where, in the film version, Bella and Edward dance

to the hauntingly beautiful song by Iron and Wine, "Flightless Bird, American Mouth," which Kirsten Stewart suggested to film director Catherine Hardwicke.

Our first view in the film of The View Point Inn comes when Edward and Bella park in front of the Inn and emerge from his silver Volvo. It's dusk and a string of lights trim the Inn. Their classmates in formal wear make their way around to the back, where they walk on red carpet, lit by hanging white globes that lead to an archway. A photographer snaps pictures of each couple as they momentarily pause under the archway; beyond the grounds, the Columbia River Gorge serves as a magnificent backdrop.

Everything in the book and the film adaptation is symbolized in the moment when Edward leans over and Bella leans back to await the final, forbidden "kiss," the one that will transform her into a vampire.

••

Though the movie scene is not faithful to the book in terms of its geography, it's clearly faithful in terms of emotion. And for that reason, *Twilight* fans may want to make a trek to Corbett, Oregon to recreate Bella and Edward's moment in time when they acknowledge they are soulmates, despite their differences. Mortal and immortal, Bella and Edward are at odds with each other in their respective desires. For now, though, they put aside their differences and dance the night away. They are oblivious to Victoria's presence; observing them from a second floor window, her black heart is riven by the loss of her soulmate, James. The movie ends as Victoria turns away to plot her revenge, a story to be told in *New Moon*, the second of four books in the Twilight saga.

Twilight
at
THE VIEW POINT INN

Web Resources

WEB RESOURCES

City of Forks, Washington: www.forkswashington.org

Ferries: www.wsdot.wa.gov/ferries

Forks Chamber of Commerce: www.forkswa.com (food, lodging, touring information)

Forks newspaper: www.forksforum.com

Forks statistics: www.city-data.com/city/Forks-Washington.html

Forks weather: www.forks-web.com

OFFICIAL WEBSITES

MySpace page: www.myspace.com/twilightthemovie

Stephenie Meyer website: www.stepheniemeyer.com

Stephenie Meyer MySpace page: www.myspace.com_stepheniemeyer (she has 150,030 friends)

Twilight book website: www.thetwilightsaga.com

Twilight movie website: www.twilightthemovie.com

YouTube page: www.youtube.com/officialtwilightfilm

Seattle-Tacoma Airport: www.portseattle.org/seatac

Major licensee: www.hottopic.com

Recommended fan websites

There are approximately 350 fan websites, ranked in order of popularity based on hits, at www.twilighttopsites.com.

Good places to start are www.twilightlexicon.com and www.twilightsource.com.

Reading

Twilight: The Complete Illustrated Movie Companion, by Mark Cotta Vaz. Trade paperback, 9.5 x 11 inches, 142 pages. Little, Brown and Company, 2008 • An shelf-worthy overview of the filming of *Twilight*. The selection of photos, in full color, is comprehensive, with "making of" shots and stills. An excellent companion to Catherine Hardwicke's *Director's Notebook*.

Twilight: Director's Notebook: The Story of How We Made the Movie Based on the Novel by Stephenie Meyer. Trade hardback, 5.4 x 8.4 inches, 176 pages. Little, Brown and Company, 2009. • Designed in scrapbook fashion with hand-lettering by Hardwicke, this tome is filled with candid photos, conceptual sketches of clothing, storyboards, character and scene photos, and much more. It's a quick overview of how Hardwicke conceptualized and shot the movie. The layout is visual and some of the photos are small.

Twilight, by Stephenie Meyer. Available in multiple editions (print, audio, and electronic), the edition of choice is the *Twilight* Collector's Edition, with improved production values: a red silk ribbon, upgraded paper stock, a new interior design for the chapter heads, and an illustrated slipcase. Likewise, *New Moon*, *Eclipse*, and *Breaking Dawn* are all available in multiple editions (print, audio, and electronic), but not (as yet) in Collectors Editions.

Viewing

Twilight, available in multiple formats (DVD, Blu-ray, Video on Demand, and iTunes) and multiple "exclusive" editions, the basic edition is a two-disc set. Borders adds an attractive tri-fold case that holds ten sparkling collector cards and bonus material: interviews, red carpet footage taken at

its Hollywood premiere, and an interview with Stephenie Meyer.

Another good choice is the Target edition, which adds a free, downloadable iTunes edition for your laptop and iPod, and a bonus third disc of supplementary material.

The Costco Collector's Giftset adds a box that contains a CD soundtrack (the $18.98 version), a watch, a charm bracelet, six glossy photo cards, a bookmark, and a certificate of authenticity.

LISTENING

Twilight: The Score ($18.98) is highly recommended. Carter Burwell's score is poignant and haunting, tonally suggesting Edward Cullen's angst but also the formidable landscape in which the movie is set. It was an immersive experience for me to be driving through Forks and listening to this score.

Twilight: Original Motion Picture Soundtrack is available in two editions: the CD only ($18.98) includes all the music by various artists from the movie; the expanded version ($24.98) adds bonus music and a DVD with interviews and music videos. My recommendation is to spend the extra money and get the expanded version, because Iron & Wine contributes a variant version of "Flightless Bird, American Mouth," which starts out with vocals only, then slowly adds instrumentation, until both blend together in a seamless whole—it's truly exquisite.

TOURING

Twilight Fan Trips
web: www.fantrips.travel/twilightfantrips/index.html

An experienced, thoroughly professional tour group, Twilight Fan Trips offers themed trips of interest to Twilighters: a trip to Italy to visit old-world vampires; a vampire-themed baseball adventure that culminates in a baseball tournament with some of the cast and crew of *Twilight*; and a fashion/prom party inspired by Alice Cullen's desire to dress up and party that culminates with a dance at The View Point Inn, where Bella and Edward waltzed the night away in the movie version.

The principal value of these tours is unparalleled access to selected events, locations, places, and people not available to the public. For instance, when would you *ever* have an opportunity to play "vampire baseball" with some of *Twilight*'s cast and crew? (That opportunity is yours through Beyond Boundaries Travel.)

These multi-day tours are the way to go if you want the ultimate Twilight tour. Their previous fan trips include domestic and international jaunts for fans of Harry Potter, Star Wars, Pirates of the Caribbean, and Jane Austen (one of Stephenie Meyer's favorite authors).

Why go alone when you can join a group that shares your Twilight passion?

CONVENTIONS

All the conventions are unofficial. Stephenie Meyer doesn't attend, but it does give fans an opportunity to meet fellow fans and, in most cases, meet some of the cast or crew from the Twilight films. The list of conventions is far too extensive to list here, but check www.twilightsource.com and under the heading of "Twilighters," click on "fan events" to get the most updated list of confirmed conventions.

STEPHENIE MEYER DAY

www.forkswa.com

Sponsored by the Forks Chamber of Commerce, this Twilight celebration was first held on September 13, 2008. A resounding success, drawing fans in from all over, the 2009 event has been expanded to a two-day celebration. Though Stephenie Meyer doesn't attend, up to a thousand female fans do, so it's a great opportunity to mix and hobnob with other members of Twilight fandom. (Note: Meyer's birthday is December 24, which proved awkward for a get-together date, so an alternative was selected.)

In a framed note on display at the Forks Chamber of Commerce, Stephenie Meyer expressed her appreciation to "the people on my favorite town," Forks. She handwrote: "I'm so honored that you've chosen Bella's birthday...as Stephenie Meyer Day. Thank you for being such gracious hosts for my vampires. You're wonderful!"

LODGING IN FORKS

Consult the Forks Chamber of Commerce website for more information, since there's a wide selection of motels, bed and breakfast inns, lodges, cabins, etc. Twilight fans, however, should check out the Pacific Inn Motel (www.pacificinnmotel.com), where I stayed during my first visit to Forks. Though I didn't stay in one of the six "Twilight themed" rooms, my friends Elisa Seaton and Lisa Jones did. They found it to be a memorable experience.

During the busy summer season, if you want one of these rooms, be sure to call well in advance to make a reservation, because they go quickly.

The Pacific Inn Motel is centrally located in the middle of town, the rooms are reasonably priced, there's free Internet access, and an on-site laundry room, too.

The only other "Twilight themed" room in town can be found at the Dew Drop Inn (www.dewdropinnmotel.com). Guests get a souvenir: a tee shirt that says, "I stayed in the Bella Suite."

Stephenie Meyer herself stayed at the Dew Drop Inn motel in July 2004, July 2007, and November 2008, but not in the Bella Suite.

Acknowledgments

Writing a book may be a journey, but the author can only reach the destination with the help of friends who make the passage easier. In random order, these are the folks who should step on stage and take a bow.

Artist Tim Kirk, my frequent collaborator on many of my books, drew up a map of Forks especially for this book. A fount of creativity, Tim's specific recommendations immeasurably improved this book. I'm privileged to know Tim.

Tim Underwood and Arnie Fenner of Underwood Books. I've known these two gentlemen for more years than I can remember. They truly know the fine art of book publishing.

My wife Mary, who is always my sounding board on every book project, from conception to delivery. When I go up the ladder, she goes up the ladder....

My literary agent, Scott Mendel, whose counsel is always sought, whose advice is always invaluable.

The good folks at Dazzled by Twilight, especially Annette Root, who took the time out of their busy schedules to help me in every way possible.

To Lisa Jones and Elisa Seaton, whom I met at the Forks Chamber of Commerce. Both of them patiently posed as I took staged photos. And listening to the score of *Twilight*, we drove out to La Push to walk through Jacob Black's world.

I owe a special debt of gratitude to the folks at the Forks Chamber of Commerce. On short notice, Marcia Bingham and Mike Gurling dropped everything they were doing to help me out in every way possible. I am especially grateful to Mike, who proofread the manuscript and also turned over his extensive photo files to insure we had the widest selection of photographs for this book project.

And, finally, thanks to the good people of Forks, who made me feel welcome. To them, this book is respectfully dedicated.

About the Contributors

George Beahm is a writer-photographer who specializes in companion-style books on popular culture. He has published dozens of books. His publishers include: Andrews McMeel Publishing, St. Martin's Press, Running Press, Potomac Books, and Hampton Roads Publishing. He lives with his wife Mary in Williamsburg, Virginia. His website is at www.georgebeahm.com.

Tim Kirk is a designer with extensive experience in a broad media spectrum—from book and magazine illustration to theme park and museum exhibit design. Tim's paintings based on J.R.R. Tolkien's epic fantasy *The Lord of the Rings* appeared in the 1975 Tolkien Calendar, published by Ballantine Books. His illustrations have appeared in a wide variety of books, magazines and fanzines; he has produced artwork for greeting cards, comics, web sites, jigsaw puzzles, costume design and character concepts for fantasy role playing games. He is a five-time winner of the prestigious Hugo Award for science fiction illustration. For 22 years, Tim was employed as an Imagineer by the Walt Disney Company. He contributed significantly to several major Disney theme park projects, including Epcot Center, Pleasure Island and the Disney-MGM Studio Tour (Florida), Disneyland (Anaheim) and Tokyo DisneySea—the second gated theme park for the Tokyo Disney Resort—which opened in 2001. Tim was a concept artist on *The Haunted Mansion* (2003), a Disney feature film based on the theme park attraction of the same name. In partnership with his brother and sister-in-law (also Disney veterans), Tim created Kirk Design. Incorporated in 2002, Kirk Design specializes in themed concept and exhibit design for museums, theme parks, restaurants and retail, with a strong emphasis on immersive, innovative storytelling; recently completed projects include the Science Fiction Museum and Hall of Fame in Seattle (2004), the Parsonage of Aimee Semple McPherson in Los Angeles (April, 2006), and the Center for Water Education in Hemet, California. Other clients include the Ronald Reagan Presidential Library, the Aquarium of the Pacific (Long Beach, California), Thinkwell Design and Production, and Ghirardelli

Chocolate. He has recently completed commissions for a new museum in Switzerland dedicated to J.R.R. Tolkien, scheduled to open in 2010-11.

With George Beahm, Tim has collaborated on a number of book projects, including *Caribbean Pirates, Fact, Fiction and Folklore in Harry Potter's World, Discovering the Golden Compass, Passport to Narnia, Muggles and Magic,* and *The Whimsic Alley Book of Spells.*

Tim Kirk is a third generation southern California native. He is a graduate of California State University at Long Beach, with a master's degree in illustration. He and his wife, Linda, make their home in Long Beach. His website is at www.kirkdesigninc.com.

Mike Gurling is a retired National Park Ranger from Olympic National Park, having worked for the National Park Service for 33 years and 36 with the federal government. He currently works as Visitor Center Manager for the Forks Chamber of Commerce in Forks, Washington. Mike has been a photographer since his high school days when he worked in his father's darkroom and took photography classes and in the U.S. Army when he served in Germany. The Forks Chamber of Commerce website is at www.forkswa.com.

Elisa Seaton is a native of the Pacific Northwest and works at home with her husband for MetLife Home Loans. The mother of two enchanting girls, Elisa began reading *Twilight* on the recommendation of a friend and became hooked. In four days, she raced through the Twilight saga. A shutterbug by nature, Elisa always travels with her digital camera.

Photo Credits

George Beahm: 6-10, 12-19, 21, 22, 24 (bottom), 25, 45-50, 52, 53, 55, 57, 58, 61, 62, 76-80, 82-83, 84, 87-89, 90-92, 94, 105, 112
Mike Gurling: front and back covers, 2-3, 4, 64-66, 68-71, 74, 96 (right), 98-99, 102, 107, 109, 110
Elisa Seaton: 56, 81
The Viewpoint Inn: 95, 96 (left), 97
All other uncredited photographs are courtesy of Stock Resource Ltd or are fair use product imagery.

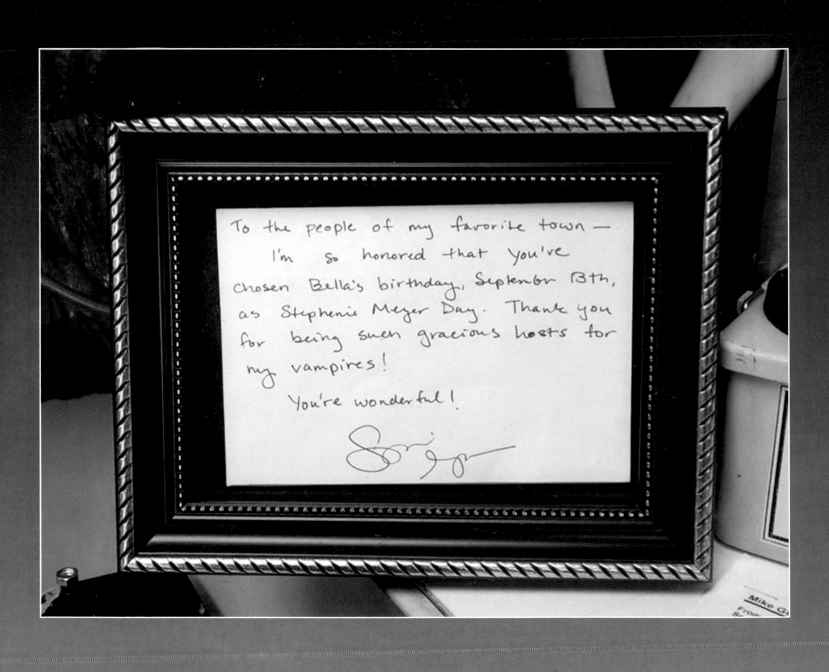

To the people of my favorite town —
I'm so honored that you've
chosen Bella's birthday, September 13th,
as Stephenie Meyer Day. Thank you
for being such gracious hosts for
my vampires!

You're wonderful!